CHORDS
for Christmas Guitar

OVER 90
CHRISTMAS CLASSICS
ALL WITH JUST 3 CHORDS!

Arranged by *Jerry Silverman*

Taylor PS-15 "Presentation Series" guitar courtesy of Taylor Guitars

Project Manager: *Aaron Stang*
Music Editor: *Colgan Bryan*
Cover Design: *Jorge Paredes*

WARNER BROS. PUBLICATIONS - THE GLOBAL LEADER IN PRINT
USA: 15800 NW 48th Avenue, Miami, FL 33014

WARNER/CHAPPELL MUSIC

CANADA: 15800 N.W. 48th AVENUE
MIAMI, FLORIDA 33014
SCANDINAVIA: P.O. BOX 533, VENDEVAGEN 85 B
S-182 15, DANDERYD, SWEDEN
AUSTRALIA: P.O. BOX 353
3 TALAVERA ROAD, NORTH RYDE N.S.W. 2113
ASIA: UNIT 901 - LIPPO SUN PLAZA
28 CANTON ROAD
TSIM SHA TSUI, KOWLOON, HONG KONG

NUOVA CARISCH

ITALY: VIA CAMPANIA, 12
20098 S. GIULIANO MILANESE (MI)
ZONA INDUSTRIALE SESTO ULTERIANO
SPAIN: MAGALLANES, 25
28015 MADRID
FRANCE: CARISCH MUSICOM,
25, RUE D'HAUTEVILLE, 75010 PARIS

INTERNATIONAL MUSIC PUBLICATIONS LIMITED

ENGLAND: GRIFFIN HOUSE,
161 HAMMERSMITH ROAD, LONDON W6 8BS
GERMANY: MARSTALLSTR. 8, D-80539 MUNCHEN
DENMARK: DANMUSIK, VOGNMAGERGADE 7
DK 1120 KOBENHAVNK

CONTENTS

Ain't That a Rocking All Night? 5

All My Heart This Night Rejoices 6

Amid the Silence 7

Angels From the Realms of Glory 8

Angels We Have Heard on High 9

As Lately We Watched 10

As With Gladness 11

The Babe of Bethlehem 12

The Boar's Head Carol 14

Bright Morning Stars 15

Bring a Torch, Jeannette, Isabella 16

Carol of the Birds 17

The Cherry Tree Carol 18

A Child This Day Is Born 19

Children, Go Where I Send Thee 20

Christ Child Lullaby 21

Christ Is Born, His Name Praise! 22

The Christ Is Coming 23

Christ Was Born on Christmas Day.......... 24

Christmas Comes Again 25

Christmas Greeting 26

Christmas Has Finally Arrived 27

Come, All Ye Shepherds.................... 28

Come, Kiss the Baby 29

Come, Let Us Adore Him 30

Come, Little Shepherds 31

Come, Thou Long Expected Jesus 32

The Coventry Carol 91

Deck the Halls 33

Ding Dong! 34

The First Noel........................... 35

The Friendly Beasts....................... 36

Glad Christmas Bells 37

Go Tell It on the Mountain................. 38

God Rest You Merry, Gentlemen............. 39

Good Christian Men, Rejoice 40

Good King Wenceslas 41

The Happy Christmas
    Comes Once More 42

Hark! The Bells Are Ringing 43

Hark! The Herald Angels Sing.............. 44

Here We Come A-Wassailing 45

The Holly Bears a Berry 46

I Heard the Bells on Christmas Day 47

I Heard-a From Heaven Today............... 48

I Saw Three Ships 49

In a Manger Was Born...................... 50

It Was Poor Little Jesus 51

It's Almost Day................................ 52

Jehovah, Hallelujah 53

Jingle Bells 54

Jolly Old St. Nicholas 55

Joy to the World 56

Lo, How a Rose E'er Blooming 57

Look-a Day 58

Mary Had a Baby 59

Mary, What You Gonna Name That
    Pretty Little Baby?...................... 60

Masters in This Hall........................ 61

Merry Christmas Bells Are Ringing 62

The New-Born Baby 63

O Come Little Children 64

O Come, O Come, Emmanuel 65

O, Jerusalem in the Morning 67

O, Mary and the Baby 68

O, Mary, Where Is Your Baby? 69

O Thou Joyful Day 66

Oh, Christmas Tree......................... 70

On Christmas Night
    All Christians Sing 71

Once in Royal David's City 72

Patapan 73

Rejoice and Be Merry 74

Rise Up, Shepherd, and Follow 75

Santa Claus Blues 76

See, Amid the Winter's Snow 77

The Seven Blessings of Mary 78

Shepherds, Shake off Your Drowsy Sleep...... 79

Shepherds to Bethlehem
    (Los Pastores a Belen) 80

Silent Night 81

Sing-a-Lamb 82

Singing in the Land 83

Sleep, My Savior, Sleep 84

The Snow Lay on the Ground 85

The Star of Christmas Morning 86

Tell Me What Month
    Was My Jesus Born In 87

There's a Song in the Air 88

Today in Bethlehem........................ 89

Tonight a Child Is Born 90

A Virgin Unspotted 4

A Visit From St. Nicholas
    (The Night Before Christmas) 92

Wasn't That a Mighty Day 94

While Shepherds Watched
    Their Flocks by Night................. 95

Yonder Comes Sister Mary 96

A Virgin Unspotted

Moderately

A___ vir - gin un - spot - ted, the___ proph - et fore - told, Should___ bring forth a___ Sav - iour, which_ we_ now be - hold; To_ be our Re - deem - er from death, hell,_ and sin, Which_ Ad - am's trans - gres - sion had_

Chorus:

wrapp'd_ us in. Aye, and there - fore be mer - ry, Set sor - row_ a - side. Christ_ Je - sus, our_ Sa - viour, was_ born_ on this tide.

The God sent an angel from heaven so high
To certain poor shepherds in fields where they lie,
And bade them no longer in sorrow to stay,
Because that our Saviour was born on this day.
(To Chorus:)

Then presently after, the shepherds did spy
Vast numbers of angels to stand in the sky.
They joyfully talked and sweetly did sing:
"To God be all glory, our heavenly King."
(To Chorus:)

To teach us humility all thus was done,
And learn we from thence haughty pride for to shun.
A manger His cradle who came from above,
The great God of mercy, of peace and of love.
(To Chorus:)

Ain't That A Rocking All Night?

Spiritual

With movement

Mar - y had_ the lit - tle Ba - by, Born in Beth - le - hem.

Ev - 'ry time_ the Ba - by cry,_ She rock in a wea - ry land.

Chorus:

Ain't that a rock - ing all night? Ain't that a rock - ing all night?_

Ain't that a rock - ing all night? All night long.

Mary bore King Jesus,
Born in Bethlehem.
Every time he Baby cry,
She rock Him in a weary land.
(To Chorus:)

Mary laid Him in the manger,
Born in Bethlehem.
Every time he Baby cry,
She rock Him in a weary land.
(To Chorus:)

All My Heart This Night Rejoices

By Paulus Gerhardt
and Horatio Parker

All my heart this night re - joic - es, As I hear far and near Sweet - est an - gel voic - es: "Christ is born." their choirs are___ sing - ing, Till the air ev - 'ry - where Now with joy is___ ring - ing.

Hark! A voice from yonder manger,
Soft and sweet doth entreat:
"Flee from woe and danger.
Brethren, come—from all that grieves you,
You are freed.
All you need I will surely give you."

Come, then, let us hasten yonder.
Here let all, great and small
Kneel in awe and wonder.
Love Him who with love is yearning.
Hail the star
That from far bright with hope is burning.

Amid The Silence

Poland

Moderately

A - mid the si - lence of the sol - emn night, Sound the glad sum - mons,

"Lo, the King of Light!" Rouse, O shep - herds, haste with sing - ing,

"Christ has come, sal - va - tion bring - ing. Born at Beth - le - hem."

Angels, From The Realm Of Glory

By James Montgomery
and Henry Smart

Shepherds, in the fields abiding,
Watching o'er your flocks by night,
God with man is now residing,
Yonder shines the infant light.
(To Chorus:)

Sages, leave your contemplations,
Brighter visions beam afar,
Seek the great Desire of nations,
Ye have seen His natal star.
(To Chorus:)

Saints before the altar bending,
Watching long in hope and fear,
Suddenly the Lord descending,
In His temple shall appear.
(To Chorus:)

Angels We Have Heard On High

Majestically

An - gels we have heard on high, Sweet - ly sing - ing o'er the plains,

And the moun - tains in re - ply Ech - o - ing their joy - ous strains.

Chorus:

Glo - ri - a

in ex - cel - sis De - o. De - o.

Shepherds, why this jubilee?
Why your joyous strains prolong?
What the gladsome tidings be
Which inspire your heav'nly song?
(To Chorus:)

Come to Bethlehem and see
Him Whose birth the angels sing;
Come, adore on bended knee,
Christ the Lord, the newborn King.
(To Chorus:)

See Him in a manger laid,
Whom the choirs of angels praise;
Mary, Joseph, lend your aid,
While our hearts in love we raise.
(To Chorus:)

As Lately We Watched

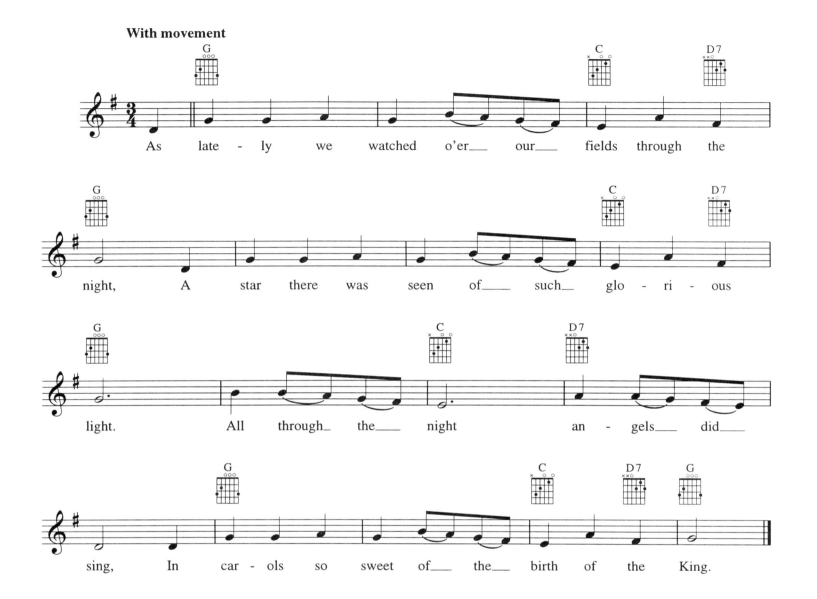

With movement

As late - ly we watched o'er__ our__ fields through the night, A star there was seen of__ such__ glo - ri - ous light. All through__ the__ night an - gels__ did__ sing, In car - ols so sweet of__ the__ birth of the King.

A King of such beauty was ne'er before seen,
And Mary, His Mother, so like to a queen.
Blest be the hour, welcome the morn,
For Christ, our dear Saviour, on earth now is born.

His throne is a mnger, His court is a loft,
But troops of bright angels, in lay, sweet and soft,
Him they proclaim, our Christ by name,
And earth, sky, and air, straight are filled with His fame.

Then shepherds, be joyful, salute your liege King,
Let hills and dales ring to the song that ye sing.
Blest be the hour, welcome the morn,
For Christ, our dear Saviour, on earth now is born.

As With Gladness

By William C. Dix
and Conrad Kocher

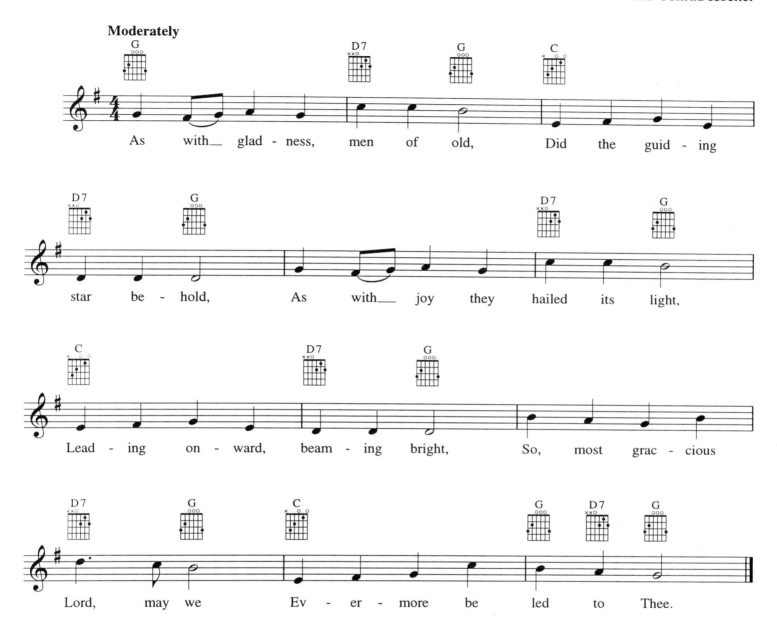

As with glad - ness, men of old, Did the guid - ing

star be - hold, As with joy they hailed its light,

Lead - ing on - ward, beam - ing bright, So, most grac - cious

Lord, may we Ev - er - more be led to Thee.

The Babe Of Bethlehem

With movement

Ye na - tions all,___ on you I call, come hear this dec - la -

ra - tion, And don't re - fuse_ this glo - r'us news of Je - sus and_ sal -

va - tion. To roy - al_ Jews came first the_ news of Christ, the great_ Mes -

si - ah, As was fore - told_ by pro - phets old, I - sa - iah, Jer - e - mi - ah.

To Abraham the promise came, and to his seed forever,
A light to shine in Isaac's line, by Scripture we discover.
Hail, promised morn! The Saviour's born, the glorious Mediator.
God's blessed word made flesh and blood, assumed the human nature.

His parents poor in earthly store, to entertain the Stranger
They found no bed to lay his head, but in the ox's manger.
No royal things, as used by kings, were seen by those who found Him,
But in the hay the Stranger lay, with swaddling bands around Him.

On the same night a glorious light to shepherds there appeared,
Bright angels came in shining flame, they saw and greatly feared.
The angles said: "Be not afraid, although we much alarm you,
We do appear, good news to bear, as now we will inform you.

The city's name is Bethlehem, in which God has appointed,
This glorious morn a Saviour's born, for Him God has anointed.
By this you'll know, if you will go, to see this little Stranger,
His lovely charms in Mary's arms, both lying in a manger."

When this was said, straightway was made a glorious sound from heaven,
Each flaming tongue an anthem sung: "To men a Saviour's given.
In Jesus' name, the glorious theme, we elevate our voices,
At Jesus birth be peace on earth, meanwhile all heaven rejoices."

Then with delight they took their flight, and wing'd their way to glory.
The shepherds gazed and were amazed, to hear the pleasing story.
To Bethlehem they quickly came, the glorious news to carry,
Ad in the stall they found them all—Joseph, the Babe, and Mary.

The shepherds then return'd again to their own habitation,
With joy of heart they did depart, now they have found salvation.
Glory, they cry, to God on high, who sent His Son to save us.
This glorious morn the Saviour's born, and his name is Christ Jesus.

The Boar's Head Carol

Moderately

The boar's head in hand bear I, Be -
decked with bays and rose - mar - y, And I pray you, my mas - ters,
mer - ry be, *Quot es - tis in con - vi - vi - o.*

Chorus:

Ca - put a - pri de - fe - ro, *Red - dens lau - des Do - mi - no.**

The boar's head I understand,
The finest dish in all the land,
Which is thus all bedecked with gay garland,
Let us *servire cantico.*
(To Chorus:)

*Be merry…I present the boar's head, give praise to God.

Bright Morning Stars

Spiritual

Don't worry about he changing meter. Just give each quarter note one beat and everything will work out fine.

Moderately, freely

Bright__ morn - ing stars are ris - ing, Bright__ morn - ing stars_ are ris - ing, Bright_ morn - ing stars are ris - ing, Day_____ is__ a - break - ing in my__ soul.

Oh, where are our dear fathers?
Oh, where are our dear fathers?
Oh, where are our dear fathers?
Day is a-breaking in my soul.

Some have gone to heaven shouting.
Some have gone to heaven shouting.
Some have gone to heaven shouting.
Day is a-breaking in my soul.

Some are down in the valley praying.
Some are down in the valley praying.
Some are down in the valley praying.
Day is a-breaking in my soul.

Some have gone to greet the Baby.
Some have gone to greet the Baby.
Some have gone to greet the Baby.
Day is a-breaking in my soul.

Bring A Torch, Jeannette, Isabella

France

Bring a torch,__ Jean - nette, Is - a - bel - la, Bring a

torch,__ come swift - ly and run. Christ is born, tell the

folk of the vil - lage. Je - sus is sleep - ing in His

cra - dle, Ah, ah. Beau - ti - ful is the

Moth - er, Ah, ah, Beau - ti - ful is her Son.

Carol Of The Birds

Slowly

Whence comes this rush of wings a - far, Fol - low - ing straight the

No - el star? Birds from the woods in won - drous flight,

Beth - le - hem seek this ho - ly night.

"Tell us, ye birds, why come ye here,
Into this stable, poor and drear?"
"Hast'ning we seek the newborn King,
And all our sweetest music bring."

Angels and shepherds, birds of the sky,
Come where the Son of God doth lie.
Christ on earth with man doth dwell,
Join in the shout, "Noël, Noël!"

The Cherry Tree Carol

When Jo - seph was an old man, an old man was_ he, He_

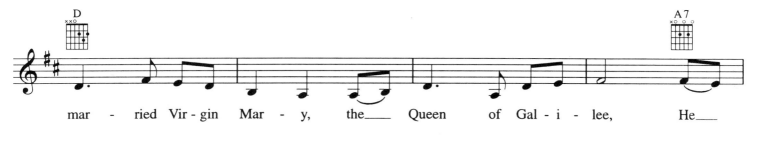

mar - ried Vir - gin Mar - y, the_ Queen of Gal - i - lee, He_

mar - ried Vir - gin Mar - y, the_ Queen of Gal - i - lee.

Then Mary spoke to Joseph,
So meek and so mild,
"Joseph, gather me some cherries,
For I am with child.
Joseph, gather me some cherries,
For I am with child."

Then Joseph grew in anger,
In anger grew he:
"Let the father of thy baby
Gather cherries for thee.
Let the father of thy baby
Gather cherries for thee."

Then Jesus spoke a few words,
A few words spoke He:
"Let my mother have some cherries,
Bow low down, cherry tree!
Let my mother have some cherries,
Bow low down, cherry tree!"

The cherry tree bowed down,
Bowed low down to the ground,
And Mary gathered cherries,
While Joseph stood around.
And Mary gathered cherries,
While Joseph stood around.

Then Joseph took Mary
All on his right knee.
"What have I done, oh, Lord?
Have mercy on me.
What have I done, oh, Lord?
Have mercy on me."

A Child This Day Is Born

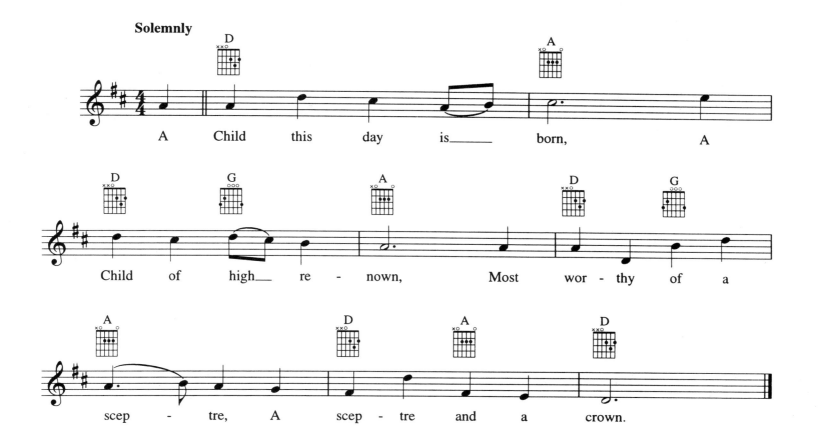

Chorus:
Nowell, Nowell, Nowell,
Nowell, sing all we may,
Because the King of all Kings
Was born this blessed day.

These tidings shepherds heard,
In field watching their fold,
Were by an angel unto them
That night revealed and told.
(To Chorus:)

And as the angel told,
So to them did appear,
They found the young child, Jesus Christ,
With Mary, His Mother dear.
(To Chorus:)

Children, Go Where I Send Thee

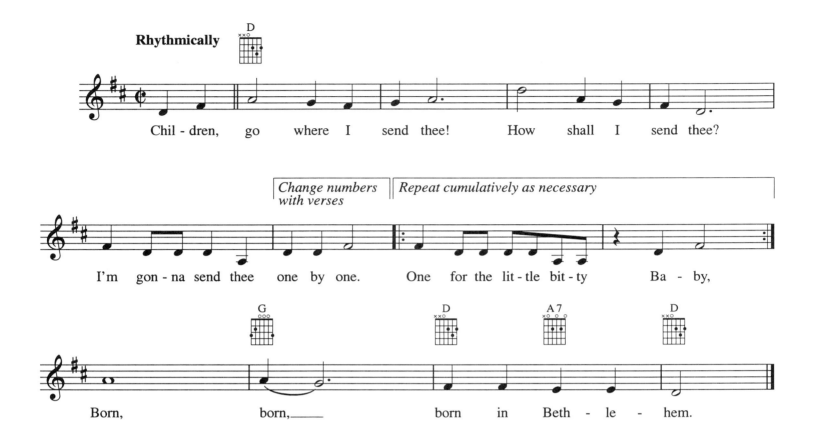

Rhythmically

Chil - dren, go where I send thee! How shall I send thee?

Change numbers with verses ‖ *Repeat cumulatively as necessary*

I'm gon - na send thee one by one. One for the lit - tle bit - ty Ba - by,

Born, born,___ born in Beth - le - hem.

Children, go where I send thee!
How shall I send thee?
I'm gonna send thee two by two:
Two for Paul and Silas,
One for the little bitty Baby,
Born, born, born in Bethlehem.

Subsequent verses follow the same pattern as verses 1 and 2, changing numbers (3, 4...)
and singing back through the verses cumulatively (2, 1; 3, 2, 1...10, 9, 8, 7, 6, 5, 4, 3, 2, 1).

…three by three: Three for the Hebrew children…
…four by four: Four for the four that stood at the door…
…five by five: Five for the Gospel preachers…
…six by six: Six for the six that never got fixed…
…seven by seven: Seven for the seven that never went to heaven…
…eight by eight: Eight for the eight that stood at the gate…
…nine by nine: Nine for the nine all dressed so fine…
…ten by ten: Ten for the Ten Commandments…

Christ Child Lullaby

The cause of talk and tale am I,
The cause of greatest fame am I.
The cause of proudest care on high,
To have for Mine the King of all.

And though You are the King of all,
They sent You to the manger stall,
Where at Your feet they all shall fall,
And glorify My Child, the King.

There shone a star above three kings,
To guide them to the King of Kings.
They held you in their humble arms,
And knelt before You until dawn.

They gave You myrrh and gave You gold,
Frankincense and gifts untold.
They traveled far these gifts to bring,
And glorify their newborn King.

Christ Is Born, His Name Praise!

Croatia

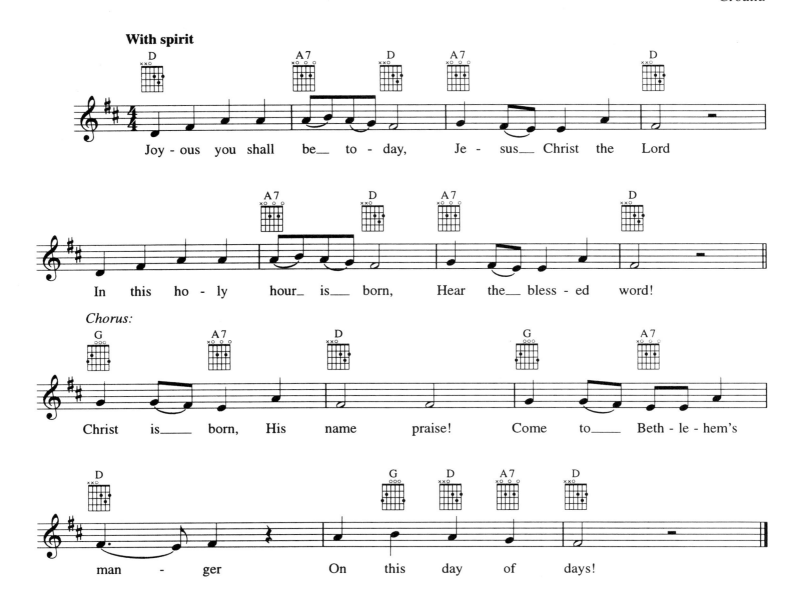

With spirit

Joy - ous you shall be— to - day, Je - sus— Christ the Lord

In this ho - ly hour— is— born, Hear the— bless - ed word!

Chorus:

Christ is— born, His name praise! Come to— Beth - le - hem's

man - ger On this day of days!

See the precious treasure there,
Lying on the straw,
Cold and naked is the Lord,
Blessed be His law!
(To Chorus:)

Maiden Mary now is crowned,
Joseph smiles with pride.
Loud hosannas angels sing
Through heaven's spaces wide.
(To Chorus:)

Lay your gifts before the Babe,
With the angels sing!
Come and greet your Saviour here,
Bless your little King!
(To Chorus:)

The Christ Is Coming

Russia

Moderately

The Christ is com - ing;___ sing His___ praise! Christ___ comes to the earth this night. The___ Christ is in heav'n, look ye at_____ Him. Sing the glo - ry of the Lord, O earth! In_____ tone the glad - ness of His praise, man - kind. Sing___ ye His glo - ry!

Christ Was Born On Christmas Day

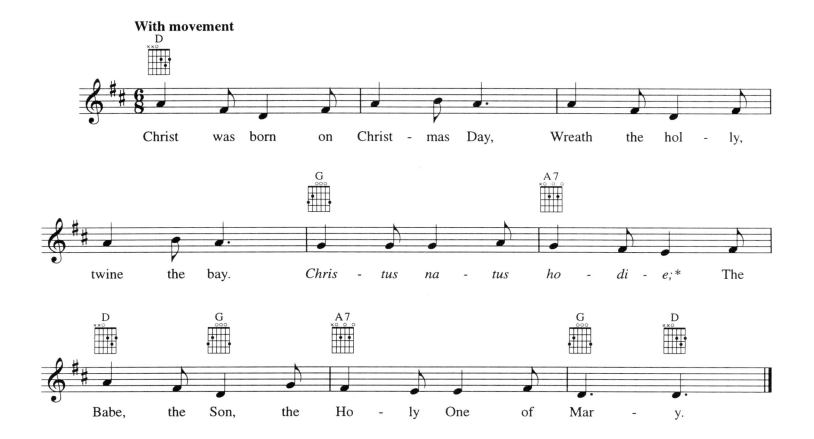

With movement

Christ was born on Christ-mas Day, Wreath the hol - ly, twine the bay. *Chris - tus na - tus ho - di - e;** The Babe, the Son, the Ho - ly One of Mar - y.

He is born to set us free,
He is born our Lord to be,
Ex Maria Virginie;**
The God, the Lord,
By all adored
Forever.

Let the bright red berries glow,
Everywhere in goodly show;
Christus natus hodie;
The Babe, the Son,
The Holy One
Of Mary.

Christian men rejoice and sing,
'Tis the birthday of a King;
Ex Maria Virginie;
The God, the Lord,
By all adored
Forever.

* Christ is born today;
** From the Virgin Mary;

Christmas Comes Again

By Rev. J. H. Hopkins

Christmas Greeting

Christmas Has Finally Arrived

Bolivian Indian

Rhythmically

Christ - mas has fi - nal-ly ar - rived, Come on, my friends, let's cel - e -

brate it. The In - fant Je - sus is a - live, Read - y to play with ev - 'ry

child. Come and a - dore Him, Come, come, come. He is our

Sav - iour, Come, come, come. Come and a - dore Him, Come, come,

come. He is our Sav - iour, Come, come, come. Oh, broth - ers, come.

Come, All Ye Shepherds

Czechoslovakia

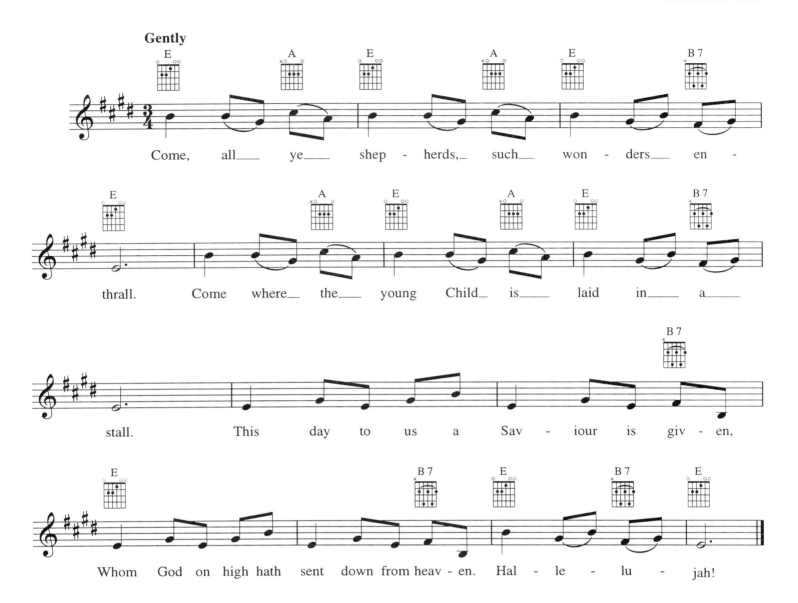

Come, all ye shep - herds, such won - ders en -
thrall. Come where the young Child is laid in a
stall. This day to us a Sav - iour is giv - en,
Whom God on high hath sent down from heav - en. Hal - le - lu - jah!

Come, hear what wonderful tidings are fraught
In Bethlehem, see what joy they have brought.
Good will from heaven to man is given,
Peace never ending to earth descending.
Glory to God!

Haste then, to Bethlehem, there to behold,
Jesus, the Babe of whom angels have told.
There to His glory tell we the story,
Glad voices raising, Him ever praising.
Hallelujah!

Come, Kiss The Baby

Portugal

Then, come, kiss the Ba - by, the beau - ti - ful

Ba - by; Then, come, kiss the Ba - by of our Bless - ed

La - dy. Then, come, kiss the Ba - by of our Bless - ed

La - dy. All the shep - herds come now to Beth - le -

hem To wor - ship the Child Who'll bring us sal - va - tion.

Come, Let Us Adore Him

Venezuela

Moderately

Come, let us a - dore Him, Shep - herds, He is ours.___

Come, let us a - dore Him, Shep - herds, He is ours.___

He lies in the man - ger, And we bring Him flow - ers,

He lies in the man - ger, And we bring Him flow - ers.

Come adore the wonder,
Trinity most holy.
Come adore the wonder,
Trinity most holy.
Though we have three Persons,
Yet, 'tis one God solely,
Though we have three Persons,
Yet, 'tis one God solely,

Came a snow-white pigeon,
Brought the news to Mary,
Came a snow-white pigeon,
Brought the news to Mary,
That within her body,
Son of God she'd carry.
That within her body,
Son of God she'd carry.

Come, Little Shepherds

Spain

Come now, lit - tle shep - herds, and come to a -

dore, The lit - tle Je - sus, Who is at the

door. Come qui - et - ly, tip - toe - ing, Don't make a

sound; The Vir - gin Ma - ri - a, the

1.

Vir - gin Ma - ri - a Is bed - ding Him

2.

down. Come bed - ding Him down._____

Come, Thou Long Expected Jesus

By Charles Wesley
and Rowland H. Prichard

Calmly

Come, Thou long___ ex - pect - ed Je - sus, Born to set Thy peo - ple free. From our fears___ and sins re - lease___ us, Let us find our rest___ in Thee. Is - rael's strength_ and con - so - la - tion, Hope of all___ the earth,___ Thou art. Dear___ De - sire___ of ev - 'ry na - tion, Joy of ev - 'ry long - ing heart.

Born thy people to deliver,
Born a Child and yet a King.
Born to reign in us forever,
Now Thy gracious kingdom bring.
By Thine own eternal Spirit
Rule in all our hearts alone.
By Thine all sufficient merit,
Raise us to Thy glorious throne.

Deck The Halls

Old English

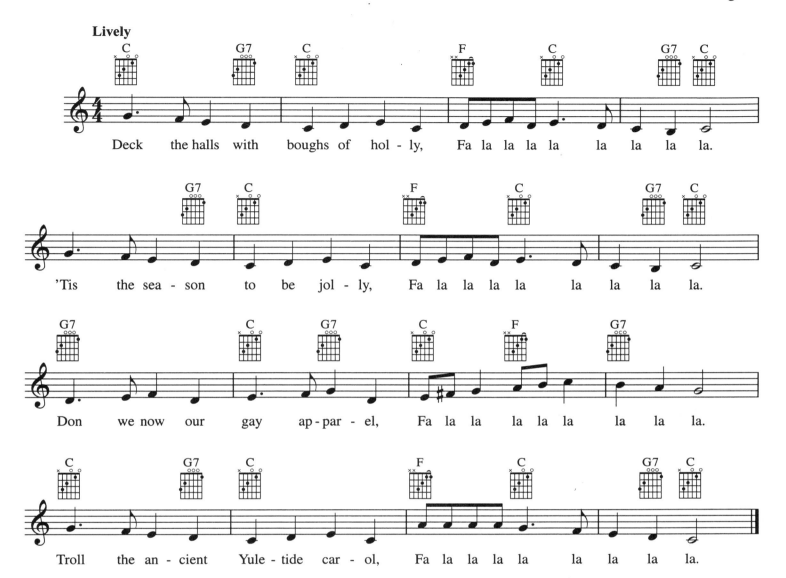

Lively

Deck the halls with boughs of hol - ly, Fa la la la la la la la la.

'Tis the sea - son to be jol - ly, Fa la la la la la la la la.

Don we now our gay ap - par - el, Fa la la la la la la la la.

Troll the an - cient Yule - tide car - ol, Fa la la la la la la la la.

See the blazing Yule before us,
Fa la la la la la la la la.
Strike the harp and join the chorus,
Fa la la la la la la la la.
Follow me in merry measure,
Fa la la la la la la la la.
While I tell of Christmas treasure,
Fa la la la la la la la la.

Fast away the old year passes,
Fa la la la la la la la la.
Hail the new! ye lads and lasses,
Fa la la la la la la la la.
Sing we joyous all together,
Fa la la la la la la la la.
Heedless of the wind and weather,
Fa la la la la la la la la.

Ding Dong!

The First Noel

Traditional English Carol

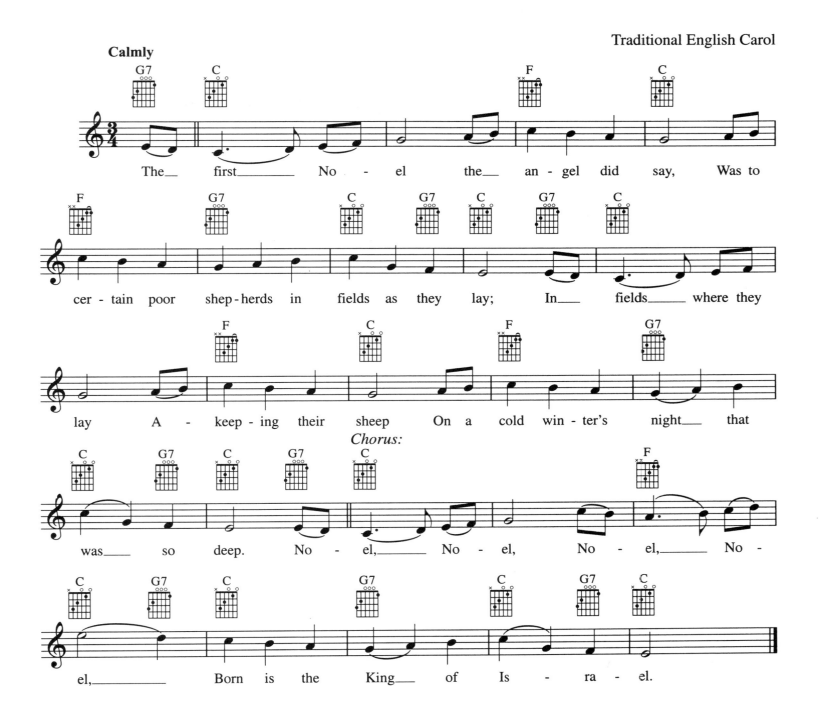

They looked up and saw a star
Shining in the East, beyond them far;
And to the earth it gave a great light,
And so it continued both day and night.
(To Chorus:)

And by the light of that same star,
Three wise men came from country far
To seek for a King was their intent,
And to follow the star wherever it went.
(To Chorus:)

This star drew nigh to the northwest,
O'er Bethlehem it took its rest;
And there it did both stop and stay,
Right over the place where Jesus lay.
(To Chorus:)

Then entered in those wise men three,
Full reverently upon their knee;
And offered there in His presence,
Their gold and myrrh and frankincense.
(To Chorus:)

The Friendly Beasts

Moderately

Je - sus, our Broth - er, kind and good, Was

hum - bly born in a sta - ble rude. And the

friend - ly beasts a - round Him stood.

Je - sus, our Broth - er, kind and good.

"I," said the donkey, shaggy and brown,
"I carried His mother up hill and down.
I carried His mother to Bethlehem town."
"I," said the donkey, shaggy and brown.

"I," said the cow all white and red,
"I gave Him my manger for His bed.
I gave Him my hay to pillow His head."
"I," said the cow all white and red.

"I," said the sheep with the curly horn,
"I gave Him my wool for His blanket warm.
He wore my coat on Christmas morn."
"I," said the sheep with the curly horn.

"I," said the dove from the rafters high,
"I cooed Him to sleep, that He would not cry.
We cooed Him to sleep, my mate and I."
"I," said the dove from the rafters high.

Glad Christmas Bells

No palace hall, its ceiling tall,
His kingly head spread over.
There only stood a stable rude,
The heavenly Babe to cover.

Nor raiment gay as there He lay,
Adorn'd the infant stranger.
Poor humble Child of mother mild,
She laid Him in a manger.

But from afar, a splendid star,
The wise men westward turning
The livelong night, saw pure and bright,
Above His birthplace burning.

Go Tell It On The Mountain

Spiritual

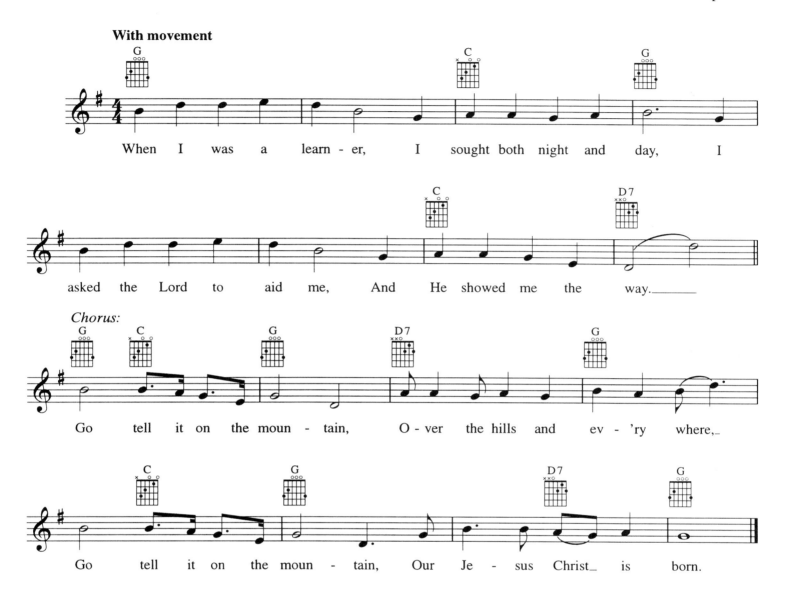

With movement

When I was a learn - er, I sought both night and day, I

asked the Lord to aid me, And He showed me the way._____

Chorus:

Go tell it on the moun - tain, O - ver the hills and ev - 'ry where,_

Go tell it on the moun - tain, Our Je - sus Christ_ is born.

While shepherds kept their watching
O'er silent flocks by night,
Behold, throughout the heavens
There shone a holy light.
(To Chorus:)

The shepherds feared and trembled,
When, lo, above the earth
Rang out the angels' chorus,
That hailed our Saviour's birth.
(To Chorus:)

Down in a lowly manger
Our humble Christ was born,
And God sent us salvation
That blessed Christmas morn.
(To Chorus:)

God Rest You Merry, Gentlemen

Traditional English Carol

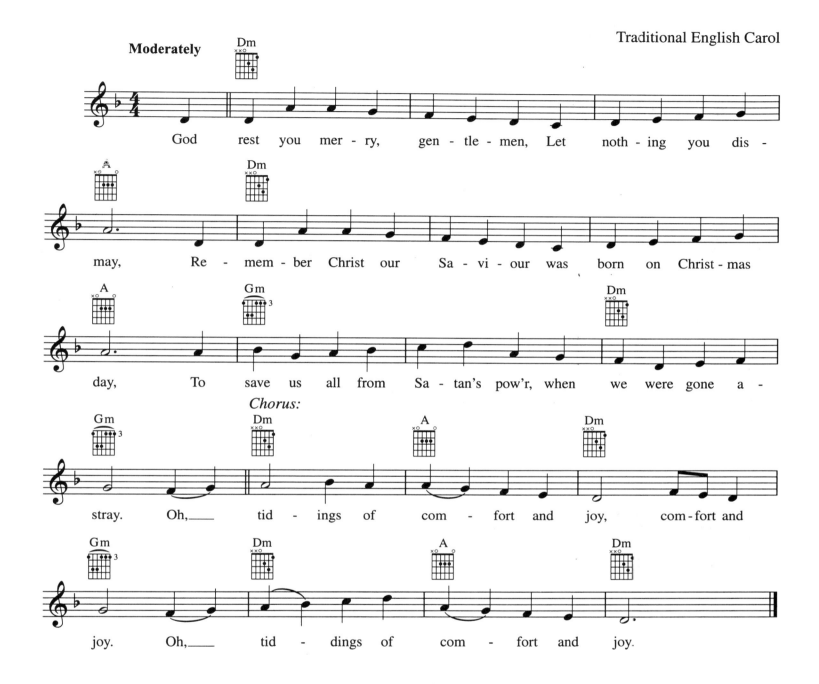

Moderately

God rest you mer - ry, gen - tle - men, Let noth - ing you dis -
may, Re - mem - ber Christ our Sa - vi - our was born on Christ - mas
day, To save us all from Sa - tan's pow'r, when we were gone a -

Chorus:

stray. Oh,___ tid - ings of com - fort and joy, com - fort and
joy. Oh,___ tid - dings of com - fort and joy.

From God, our heav'nly Father,
A blessed angel came,
And unto certain shepherds
Brought tidings of the same;
How that in Bethlehem was born
The Son of God by name.
(To Chorus:)

The shepherds at those tidings
Rejoicéd much in mind,
And left their flocks a-feeding
In tempest, storm and wind,
And went straightway to Bethlehem,
The Son of God to find.
(To Chorus:)

And when they came to Bethlehem,
Where our dear Saviour lay,
They found Him in a manger,
Where oxen feed on hay.
His mother Mary kneeling down,
Unto the Lord did pray.
(To Chorus:)

Now to the Lord sing praises,
All you within this place,
And with true love and brotherhood
Each other now embrace.
This holy tide of Christmas
All others do deface.
(To Chorus:)

Good Christian Men, Rejoice

Germany

With movement

Good Chris - tian men, re - joice_____ with heart and soul and

voice._____ Give ye heed to what we say: "News! News!

Je - sus Christ is born to - day! Ox and ass be -

fore Him bow, And He is in the man - ger now.

Christ is born to day!_____ Christ is born to - day.

Good Christian men, rejoice
With heart and soul and voice.
Now year hear of endless bliss.
Joy! Joy! Jesus Christ was born for this.
He hath ope'd the heav'nly door,
And man is blessed for evermore.
Christ was born for this.
Christ was born for this.

Good Christian men, rejoice
With heart and sould and voice.
Now ye need not fear the grave.
Peace!, Peace! Jesus Christ was born to save.
Calls you one and calls you all,
To gain His everlasting hall.
Christ was born to save.
Christ was born to save.

Good King Wenceslas

Traditional English Carol

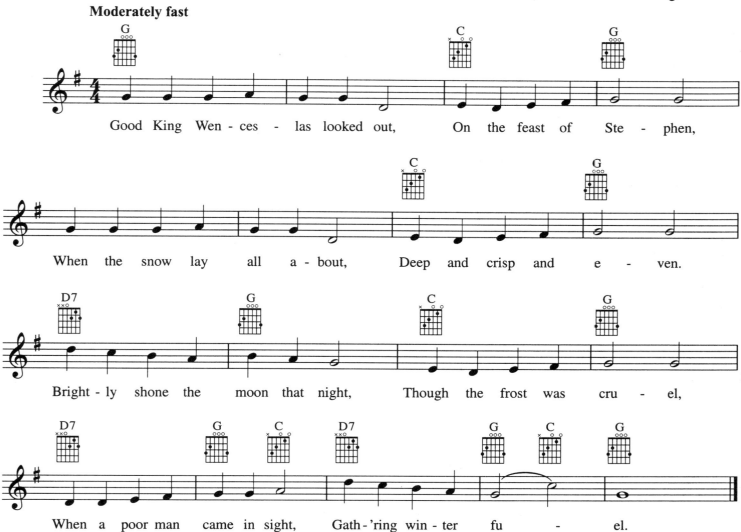

Moderately fast

Good King Wen - ces - las looked out, On the feast of Ste - phen,

When the snow lay all a - bout, Deep and crisp and e - ven.

Bright - ly shone the moon that night, Though the frost was cru - el,

When a poor man came in sight, Gath - 'ring win - ter fu - el.

"Hither, page, and stand by me,
If thou know'st it telling.
Yonder peasant, who is he?
Where and what his dwelling?"
"Sire, he lives a good league hence,
Underneath the mountain,
Right against the forest fence,
By Saint Agnes' fountain."

"Bring me flesh and bring me wine,
Bring me pine logs hither.
Thou and I shall see him dine,
When we bear them thither."
Page and monarch, forth they went,
Forth they went together;
Through the rude wind's wild lament,
And the bitter weather.

"Sire, the night is darker now,
And the wind grows stronger.
Fails my heart, I know not how;
I can go no longer."
"Mark my footsteps, my good page,
Tread thou in them boldly.
Thou shalt find the winter's rage
Freeze they blood less coldly."

In his master's steps he trod,
Where the snow lay dinted.
Heat was in the very sod,
Which the Saint had printed.
Therefore, Christian men, be sure,
Wealth or rank possessing,
Ye who now will bless the poor,
Shall yourselves find blessing.

0458B

The Happy Christmas Comes Once More

By Nicolai Gruntvig,
C. P. Krauth and C. Balle

Hark! The Bells Are Ringing

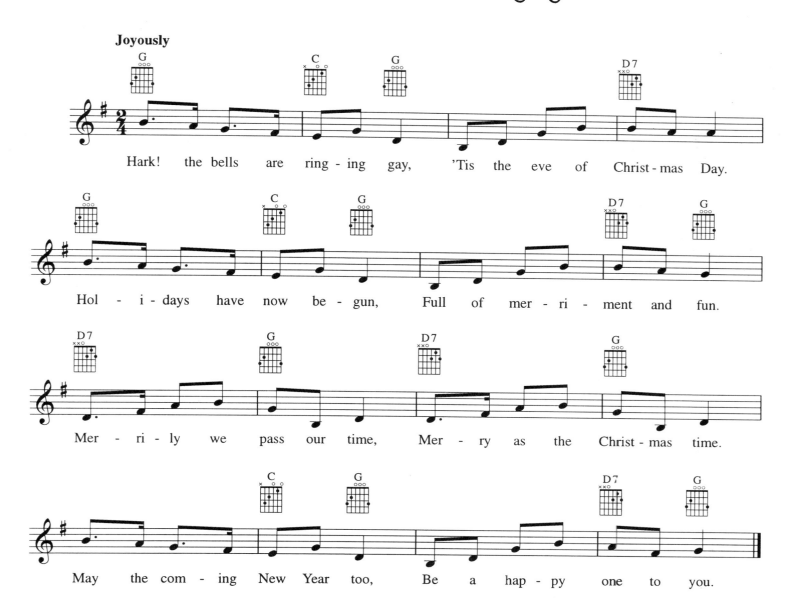

Joyously

Hark! the bells are ring - ing gay, 'Tis the eve of Christ - mas Day.

Hol - i - days have now be - gun, Full of mer - ri - ment and fun.

Mer - ri - ly we pass our time, Mer - ry as the Christ - mas time.

May the com - ing New Year too, Be a hap - py one to you.

Hark! The Herald Angels Sing

Words by Charles Wesley
Music by Felix Mendelssohn

Majestically

Hark! the her - ald an - gels sing, "Glo - ry to the new - born King!

Peace on earth, and mer - cy mild,__ God and sin - ners re - con - ciled."

Joy - ful all ye na - tions rise,__ Join in tri - umph of the skies;__

With th'an - gel - ic host pro - claim, "Christ is__ born in Beth - le - hem."

Hark! the her - ald an - gels sing, "Glo - ry__ to the new - born King!"

Christ, by highest heaven adored;
Christ, the everlasting Lord!
Late in time behold him come,
Offspring of the Virgin's womb.
   Veiled in flesh the Godhead, see;
   Hail th'incarnate Deity.
   Pleased as man with men to dwell,
   Jesus, our Emmanuel.
Hark! the herald angels sing,
"Glory to the newborn King!"

Hail, the heaven-born Prince of Peace!
Hail, the Sun of Righteousness!
Light and life to all He brings,
Risen with healing in his wings
   Mild He lays His glory by;
   Born that man no more may die.
   Born to raise the sons of earth;
   Born to give them second birth.
Hark! the herald angels sing,
"Glory to the newborn King!"

Here We Come A-Wassailing

We are not daily beggars
That beg from door to door,
But we are neighbors' children,
Whom you have seen before.
(To Chorus:)

We have got a little purse
Of stretching leather skin.
We want a little money,
To line it well within.
(To Chorus:)

Bring us out a table,
And spread it with a cloth.
Bring us out a mouldy cheese,
And some of your Christmas loaf.
(To Chorus:)

God bless the master of this house,
Likewise the mistress too;
And all the little children,
That 'round the table go.
(To Chorus:)

The Holly Bears A Berry

Oh, the holly bears a berry that's green as the grass.
Mary bore Jesus who died on the cross.
(To Chorus:)

Oh, the holly bears a berry, as blood it is red.
Mary bore Jesus who died in our stead.
(To Chorus:)

Oh, the holly bears a berry as black as the coal.
Mary bore Jesus who died for us all.
(To Chorus:)

I Heard The Bells On Christmas Day

By Henry W. Longfellow
and J. Baptiste Calkin

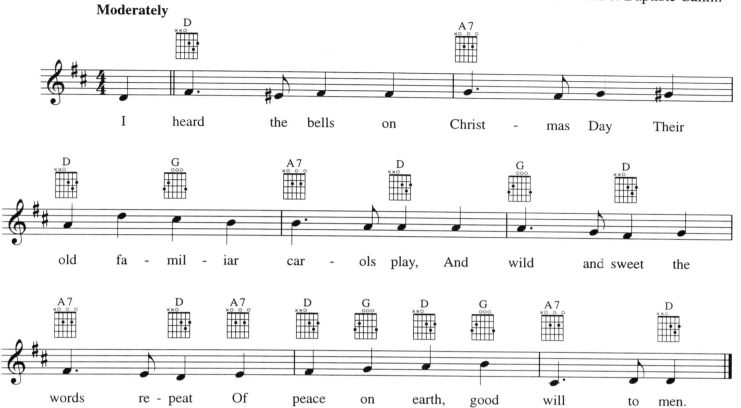

I thought how, as the day had come,
The belfries of all Christendom
Had roll'd along the unbroken song
Of peace on earth, good will to men.

And in despair I bow'd my head:
"There is no peace on earth," I said,
"For hate is strong, and mocks the song
Of peace on earth, good will to men."

Then pealed the bells more loud and deep:
"God is not dead, nor doth he sleep;
The wrong shall fail, the right prevail,
With peace on earth, good will to men."

I Heard-a From Heaven Today

Spiritual

With movement

Chorus:

Hur - ry on, my wea - ry soul, And I heard - a from heav - en to -

Fine

day. Hur - ry on, O, my wea - ry soul, And I heard-a from heav - en to - day.

Verse:

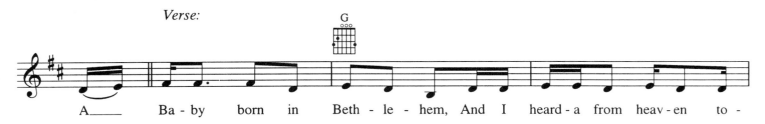

A____ Ba - by born in Beth - le - hem, And I heard - a from heav - en to -

day. A Ba - by born in___ Beth - le - hem, And I heard-a from heav - en to - day.

The bell is a-ringing in the other bright world,
    And I heard-a from heaven today.
The bell is a-ringing in the other bright world,
    And I heard-a from heaven today.
(To Chorus:)

The angels a-singing in the heavenly band,
    And I heard-a from heaven today.
The angels a-singing in the heavenly band,
    And I heard-a from heaven today.
(To Chorus:)

The trumpet sounds in the other land,
    And I heard-a from heaven today.
The trumpet sounds in the other land,
    And I heard-a from heaven today.
(To Chorus:)

I Saw Three Ships

Traditional English Carol

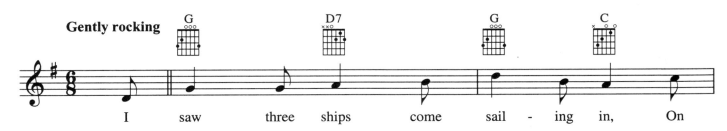

I saw three ships come sail - ing in, On

Christ - mas day, on Christ - mas day. I saw three ships come

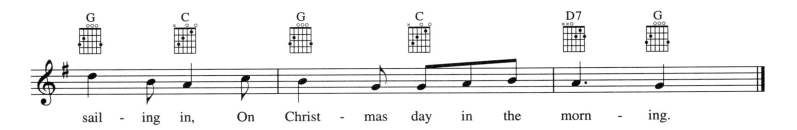

sail - ing in, On Christ - mas day in the morn - ing.

And what was in those ships all three,
On Christmas day, on Christmas day?
And what was in those ships all three,
On Christmas day in the morning?

The Virgin Mary and Christ were there,
On Christmas day, on Christmas day.
The Virgin Mary and Christ were there,
On Christmas day in the morning.

In A Manger Was Born

Chile

It Was Poor Little Jesus

Spiritual

It was poor_ lit - tle Je - sus, yes, yes,_

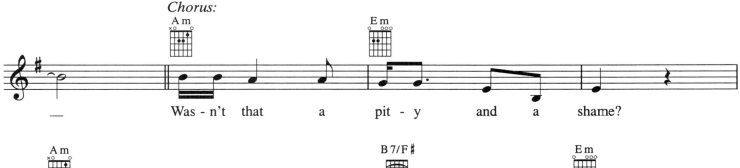

_ He was born_ on_ Christ - mas, yes, yes,_

_ And he laid_ in a man - ger, yes, yes.

Chorus:

_ Was - n't that a pit - y and a shame?

Lord, Lord,_ Was - n't that a pit - y and a shame?_

It was poor little Jesus, yes, yes,
Child of Mary, yes, yes,
Didn't have no cradle, yes, yes.
(To Chorus:)

It was poor little Jesus, yes, yes,
They took Him from His manger, yes, yes,
They took Him from His mother, yes, yes.
(To Chorus:)

It was poor little Jesus, yes, yes,
They bound Him with a halter, yes, yes,
And whipped Him up the mountain, yes, yes.
(To Chorus:)

It was poor little Jesus, yes, yes,
They nailed Him to the cross, Lord, yes, yes,
They hung Him with a robber, yes, yes.
(To Chorus:)

It was poor little Jesus, yes, yes,
He's risen from the darkness, yes, yes,
He's ascended into glory, yes, yes.
(To Chorus:)

It was poor little Jesus, yes, yes,
He was born on a Friday, yes, yes,
He was born on Christmas, yes, yes.
(To Chorus:)

It's Almost Day

Spiritual

Lively

Chick - ens crow - ing for mid - night, And it's al - most day.

Chick - ens crow - ing for mid - night, And it's al - most day.

Thought I heard my moth - er say, It's al - most day.

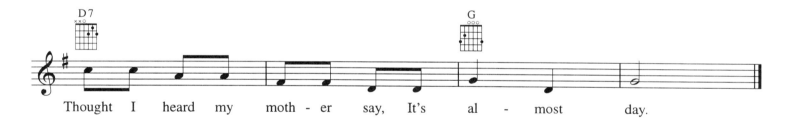

Thought I heard my moth - er say, It's al - most day.

Think I heard my papa say,
It's almost day.
Think I heard my papa say,
It's almost day.
(To Chorus:)

Christmas is a-coming,
And it's almost day.
Christmas is a-coming,
And it's almost day.
(To Chorus:)

Children are all happy
On Christmas day.
Children are all happy
On Christmas day.
(To Chorus:)

Santa Claus is coming,
And it's almost day.
Santa Claus is coming,
And it's almost day.
(To Chorus:)

Jehovah, Hallelujah

Spiritual

With movement

Chorus:

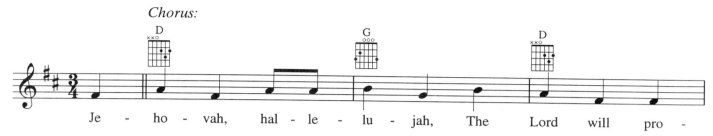

Je - ho - vah, hal - le - lu - jah, The Lord will pro -

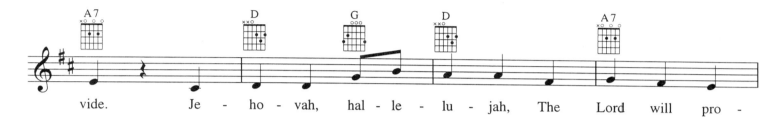

vide. Je - ho - vah, hal - le - lu - jah, The Lord will pro -

Fine   *Verse:*

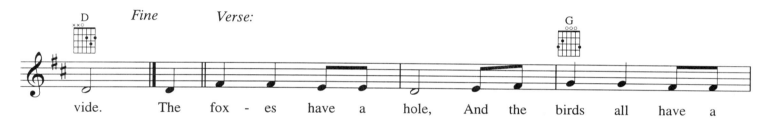

vide. The fox - es have a hole, And the birds all have a

nest. The Son of God He___ dun - no where to take His wea - ry rest.

The animals they came
From far and from near,
To witness the birth
Of the Baby so dear.
(To Chorus:)

The sweet little Babe,
Lying there on the straw;
The greatest of miracles
The world ever saw.
(To Chorus:)

Jingle Bells

Jingle Bells has four chords—but we just couldn't leave it out.

By J. Pierpont

A day or two ago,
I thought I'd take a ride,
And soon Miss Fannie Bright
Was seated by my side.
The horse was lean and lank,
Misfortune seemed his lot.
He got into a drifted bank,
And then we got upsot.
(To Chorus:)

Jolly Old St. Nicholas

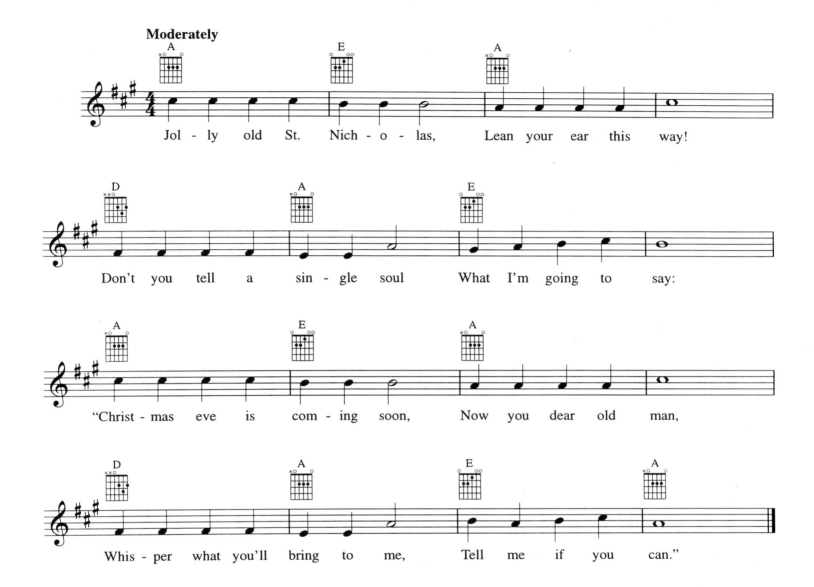

"When the clock is striking twelve,
When I'm fast asleep,
Down the chimney broad and black,
With your pack you'll creep.
All the stockings you will find
Hanging in a row.
Mine will be the shortest one,
You'll be sure to know."

Joy To The World

Words by Isaac Watts
Music by George F. Handel

Joy to the world! the Lord is come, Let earth re - ceive her King._____ Let ev - 'ry__ heart____ pre - pare__ Him__ room,____ And heav'n and na - ture_ sing, And_ heav'n and na - ture_ sing, And_ heav - en, and heav - en and na - ture sing.

Joy to the world! the Saviour reigns;
Let men their songs employ,
While fields and floods,
And rocks, hills and plains
Repeat the sounding joy,
Repeat the sounding joy,
Repeat, repeat the sounding joy.

He rules the world with truth and grace,
And makes the nations prove
The glories of
His righteousness,
The wonders of his love,
The wonders of his love,
The wonders, the wonders of his love.

Lo, How A Rose E'er Blooming

By Michael Prætorious

Moderately

Lo, how a rose e'er bloom - ing, From ten - der stem___

___ has sprung! Of Jes - se's lin - eage com - ing, As

men of old___ have sung. It came, a flow'r - et bright,

A - mid the cold of win - ter, When half - spent was___ the night.

Isaiah 'twas foretold it,
The Rose I have in mind.
With Mary we behold it,
The Virgin Mother kind,
To show God's love aright,
She bore to men a Saviour,
When half-spent was the night.

Look-a Day

Spiritual

With movement

True be - liev - er, O, o, look - a day. Day de com - in',

O, o, look - a day. Look - a day, look - a day, Day de com - in'.

Look - a day, look - a day, Day de com - in'. True be - liev - er,

O, o, look - a day. Day de com - in', O, o, look - a day.

Morning starlight,
   O, o, look-a day.
Day de comin',
   O, o, look-a day.
Looka-day, look-a day,
Jump like a member.
Looka-day, look-a day,
Hop like a member.
True believer,
   O, o, look-a day.
True believer,
   O, o, look-a day.

Mary Had A Baby

Spiritual

Rhythmically

Mar - y had a Ba - by, Oh, Lord.— Mar - y had a Ba - by,

Oh, my— Lord. Mar - y had a Ba - by, Oh, Lord.— The

peo - ple keep a - com - ing and the train— done gone.

What did she name Him?
  Oh, Lord.
She called Him Jesus,
  Oh, my Lord.
Where was He born?
  Oh, Lord.
The people keep a-coming and the train done gone.

Born in a stable,
  Oh, Lord.
Where did they lay Him?
  Oh, my Lord.
Laid Him in a manger,
  Oh, Lord.
The people keep a-coming and the train done gone.

Mary, What You Gonna Name That Pretty Little Baby?

Spiritual

Mary, what you gonna name that pretty little Baby?
  Mmm, pretty little Baby,
  Mmm, laid Him in a manger.
Glory be to the newborn King.

Some call Him one thing, I think I'll call Him Jesus.
  Mmm, pretty little Baby,
  Mmm, laid Him in a manger.
Glory be to the newborn King.

Some call Him one thing, I think I'll call Him Emmanuel.
  Mmm, pretty little Baby,
  Mmm, laid Him in a manger.
Glory be to the newborn King.

Some call Him one thing, I think I'll call Him Saviour.
  Mmm, pretty little Baby,
  Mmm, laid Him in a manger.
Glory be to the newborn King.

Masters In This Hall

This song has four chords—but we just couldn't leave it out.

Masters in this hall,_____ Hear ye news to-day,_____
Brought from o - ver sea, And ev - er I you pray.

Chorus:

Now - ell, Now - ell, Now - ell! Now - ell, sing we clear! Hol - pen are all folk on
Now - ell, Now - ell, Now - ell! Now - ell, sing we loud! God to - day hath all folk

earth,___ Born___ is God's son so dear. cast a - down the proud.
raised___ And___

Then to Bethl'em town
We went two and two.
In a sorry place
We heard the oxen low.
(To Chorus:)

Ox and ass Him know,
Kneeling on their knee.
Wondrous joy and I,
This little Babe to see.
(To Chorus:)

This is Christ, the Lord,
Masters, be ye glad!
Christmas has come in,
And no folk should be sad.
(To Chorus:)

Merry Christmas Bells Are Ringing

By M. E. White
and H. Kotzschman

Lively

Mer - ry Christ - mas bells are ring - ing, Ring - ing__ far and__ near.

An - gel voic - es sweet - ly sing - ing, Sing - ing__ soft__ and__ clear:

"Glo - ry, for the Lord__ is__ come. Je - sus makes____ the earth His home."

Happy voices catch the echo
Of the angels' song.
Grand old chant and joyous carol
Ring the aisles along.
Let our lips their homage pay
To the Saviour born today.

And have we no gifts to offer
To our Lord and King?
Lord, ourselves, heart, soul and body,
Unto Thee we bring.
With our lives glad homage pay
To the Saviour, born today!

0458B

The Newborn Baby

Spiritual

Moderately

Ba - by born in Beth - le - hem, O, when I get in glo - ry.

O, when I get in glo - ry, Glo - ry be to the new - born

Chorus:

Ba - by._____ World reel when I get in glo - ry.

O, when I get in glo - ry. O, when I get in glo - ry.

Glo - ry be to the new - born Ba - by._____

Born to set the people free,
O, when I get in glory.
O, when I get in glory.
Glory be to the newborn Baby.
(To Chorus:)

Born to be the King of Kings,
O, when I get in glory.
O, when I get in glory.
Glory be to the newborn Baby.
(To Chorus:)

O Come, Little Children

By Christoph von Schmid
and J. A. P. Schulz

The hay is His pillow, the manger His bed.
The beasts stand in wonder to gaze on His head.
Yet there where He lieth, so weak and so poor,
Come shepherds and wise men to kneel at His door.

Now "Glory to God!" sing the angels on high.
And "Peace upon earth!" heav'nly voices reply.
Then, come little children, amd join in the lay
That gladdened the world on the first Christmas day.

0458B

O Come, O Come, Emmanuel

By Thomas Helmore

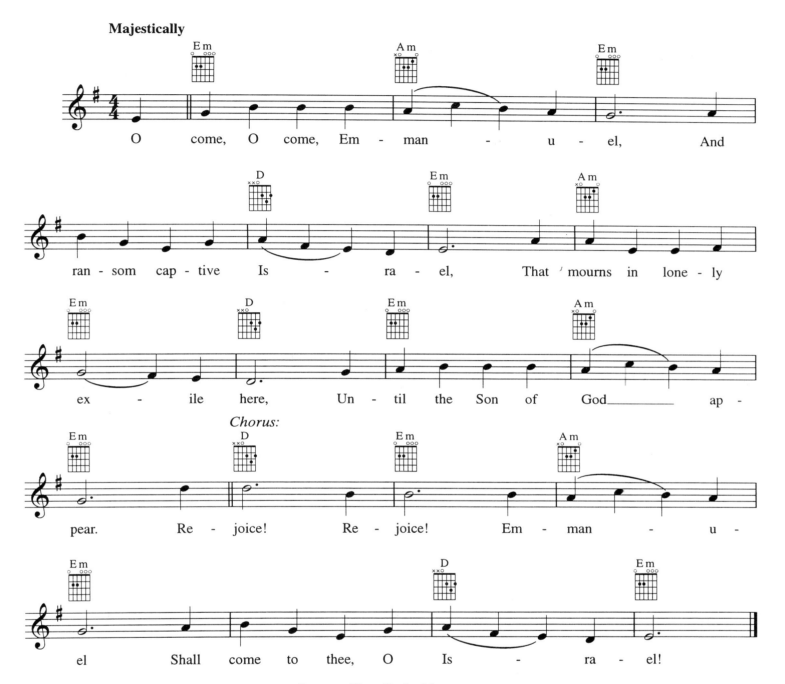

O come, Thou Rod of Jesse,
Free Thine own from Satan's tyranny.
From depths of hell Thy people save,
And give them victory o'er the grave.
(To Chorus:)

O come, Thou Dayspring, come and cheer
Our spirits by Thine advent here,
And drive away the shades of night,
And pierce the clouds and bring us light.
(To Chorus:)

O come, Thou Key of David, come,
And open wide our heavenly home.
Make safe the way that leads on high,
And close the path to misery.
(To Chorus:)

O Thou Joyful Day

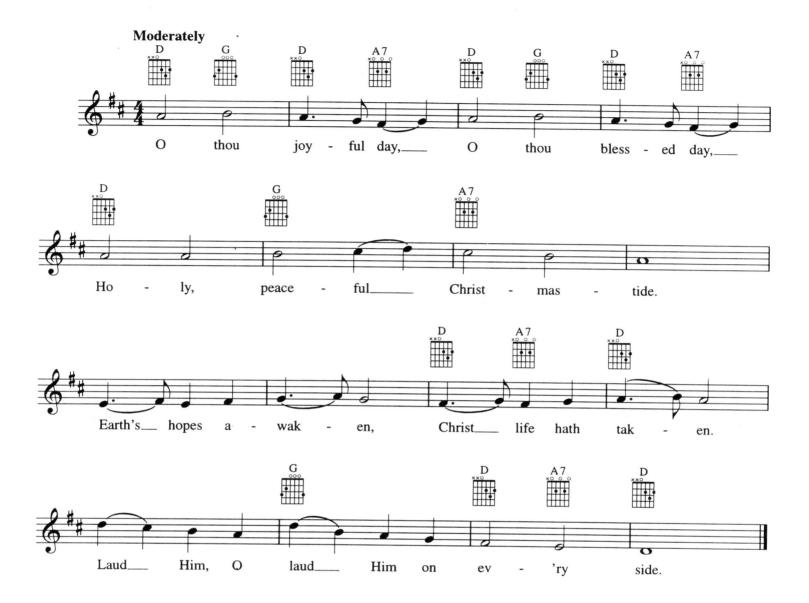

O, Jerusalem In The Morning

Traditional

With movement

Moth - er Mar - y, what is the mat - ter? O, Je - ru - s'lem in the morn - ing.

Moth - er Mar - y, what is the mat - ter? O, Je - ru - s'lem in the morn - ing.

Chorus:

Ba - by born to - day,___ O, Je - ru - s'lem in the morn - ing.

Born___ in the man - ger, O, Je - ru - s'lem in the morn - ing.

Father Joseph, what is the matter?
  O, Jerus'lem in the morning.
Father Joseph, what is the matter?
  O, Jerus'lem in the morning.
(To Chorus:)

All wrapped up in swaddling clothing.
  O, Jerus'lem in the morning.
All wrapped up in swaddling clothing.
  O, Jerus'lem in the morning.
(To Chorus:)

Manger was His cradle.
  O, Jerus'lem in the morning.
Manger was His cradle.
  O, Jerus'lem in the morning.
(To Chorus:)

Born in Bethlehem.
  O, Jerus'lem in the morning.
Born in Bethlehem.
  O, Jerus'lem in the morning.
(To Chorus:)

O, Mary And The Baby

Spiritual

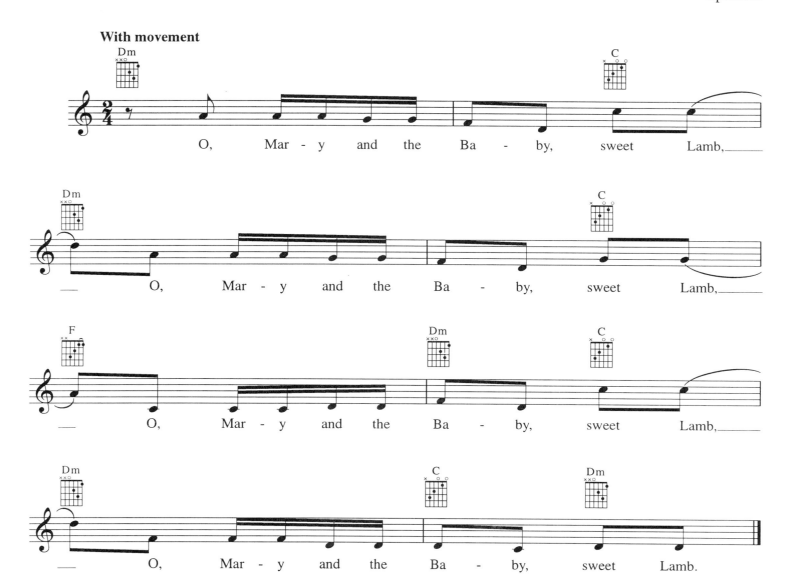

It's a holy Baby, sweet Lamb…(3)
O, Mary and the Baby, sweet Lamb.

I love that Baby, sweet Lamb…(3)
O, Mary and the Baby, sweet Lamb.

It's a God-sent Baby, sweet Lamb…(3)
O, Mary and the Baby, sweet Lamb.

Come see the baby, sweet Lamb…(3)
O, Mary and the Baby, sweet Lamb.

It's a beautiful Baby, sweet Lamb…(3)
O, Mary and the Baby, sweet Lamb.

It's Mary's Baby, sweet Lamb…(3)
O, Mary and the Baby, sweet Lamb.

O, Mary, Where Is Your Baby?

Spiritual

Yes, it has four chords—but E and E7 are so similar!

With movement

Read in the gos-pel of Math-a-yew,_ The gos-pel of Luke and John,

Read in the gos-pel and learn the news,_ How the li'l boy child was born.

Read a-bout Mar-y and Jo - seph,_ come a-rid-ing on a don-key from far.

Slept in the sta-ble of Beth-le-hem,_ Where the shep-herds all seen the star.

Chorus:

O,_____ Mar - y, Where is your Ba - by? They done

took Him from a man-ger, And car-ried Him to the throne.

Read about the elders and the Hebrew priest,
A-preaching in the tabernacle hall;
Standing in a-wonder at the words they heard
From a li'l boy child so small.
"O, li'l boy, how old you is?
Tell it if you let it be told.
O, li'l boy, how old you is?"
"I ain't but twelve years old."
(To Chorus:)

Oh, Christmas Tree

Germany: "Oh, Tannenbaum"

Oh, Christmas tree, oh, Christmas tree,
Of all the trees most lovely. } (2)
Each year you bring to me delight,
Gleaming in the Christmas night.
Oh, Christmas tree, oh, Christmas tree,
Of all the trees most lovely.

Oh, Christmas tree, oh, Christmas tree,
Your leaves will teach me also, } (2)
That hope and love and faithfulness
Are precious things I can possess.
Oh, Christmas tree, oh, Christmas tree,
Your leaves will teach me also.

On Christmas Night All Christians Sing

Once In Royal David's City

By C. F. Alexander
and H. J. Gauntlett

Moderately

Once in roy - al Da - vid's__ cit - y Stood a low - ly cat - tle__ shed, Where a moth - er laid__ her__ Ba - by In a man - ger for__ His__ bed. Mar - y was that moth - er mild, Je - sus Christ her lit - tle__ Child.

Patapan

France

When the men of olden days
Gave the King of Kings their praise,
They had pipes on which to play,
Turelurelu, patapatapan.
They had drums on which to play,
Full of joy on Christmas Day.

God and man this day become
Joined as one with flute and drum.
Let the happy tune play on,
Turelurelu, patapatapan.
Flute and drum together play,
As we sing on Christmas Day.

Rejoice And Be Merry

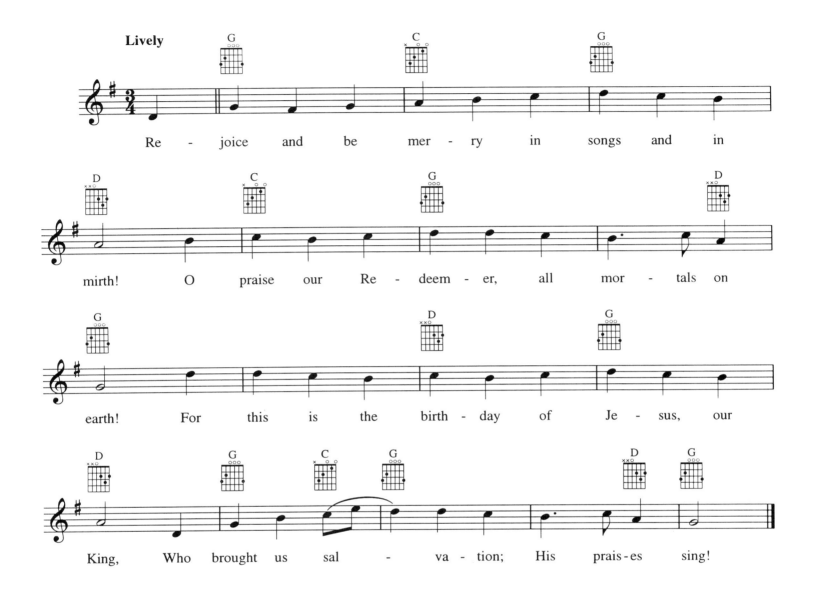

Re - joice and be mer - ry in songs and in mirth! O praise our Re - deem - er, all mor - tals on earth! For this is the birth - day of Je - sus, our King, Who brought us sal - va - tion; His prais - es sing!

A heavenly vision appeared in the sky;
Vast numbers of angels the shepherds did spy,
Proclaiming the birthday of Jesus, our King,
Who brought us salvation—His praises we'll sing!

Likewise a bright star in the sky did appear,
Which led the wise men from the east to draw near.
They found the Messiah, sweet Jesus, our King,
Who brought us salvation—His praises we'll sing!

Rise Up, Shepherd, And Follow

Spiritual

If you take good heed to the angel's words,
Rise up, shepherd, and follow,
You'll forget your flocks, you'll forget your herds,
Rise up, shepherd, and follow.
(To Chorus:)

0458B

Santa Claus Blues

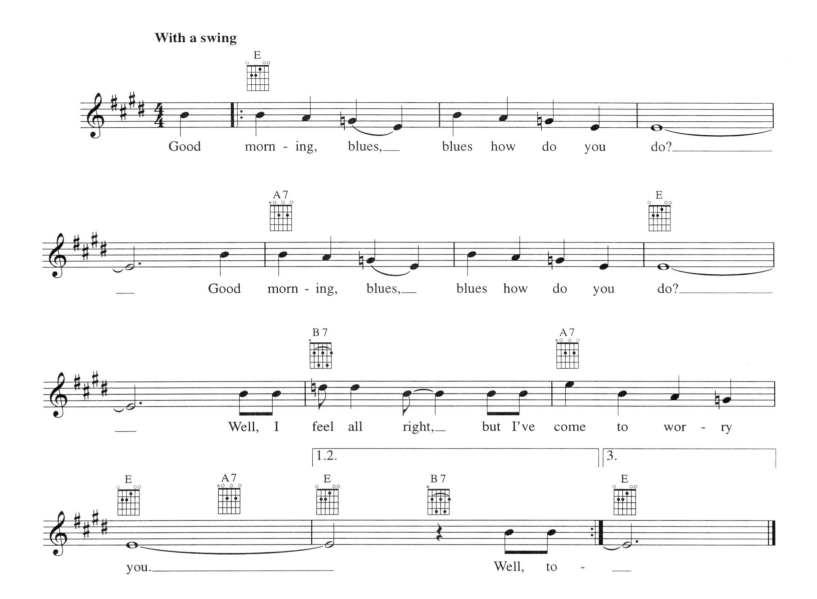

Well, tomorrow's Christmas and I want to see Santa Claus,
Well, tomorrow's Christmas and I want to see Santa Claus,
If I don't get my baby for Christmas, gonna break all the laws.

Santy Claus, Santy Claus, just listen to my plea,
Santy Claus, Santy Claus, just listen to my plea,
I don't want nothin' for Christmas but my baby back to me.

See, Amid The Winter's Snow

By John Goss

Lo, within a manger lies
He, who built the starry skies.
He, who throned in height sublime,
Sits among the cherubim.
(To Chorus:)

As we watched in dead of night,
Lo, we saw a wondrous light:
Angels singing peace on earth,
Told us of our Saviour's birth.
(To Chorus:)

Teach, O teach us, holy Child,
By Thy face so meek and mild,
Teach us to resemble Thee,
In Thy sweet humility.
(To Chorus:)

The Seven Blessings Of Mary

Moderately

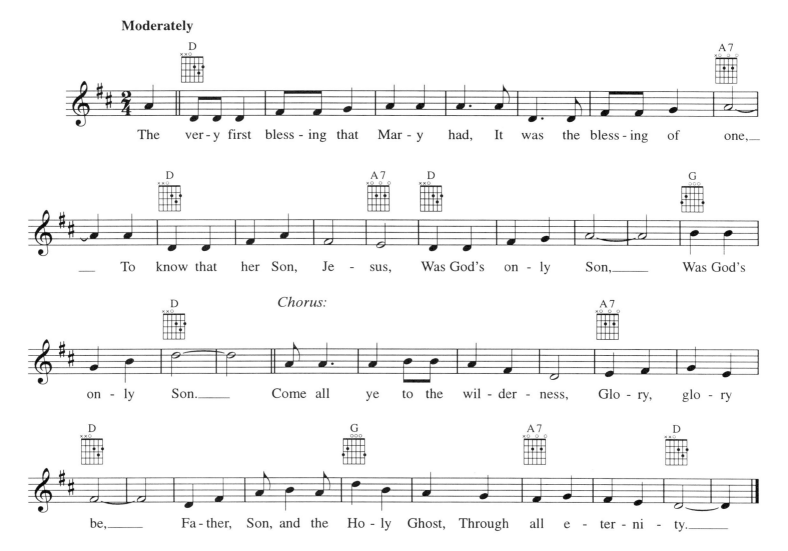

The ver-y first bless-ing that Mar-y had, It was the bless-ing of one,___

___ To know that her Son, Je - sus, Was God's on - ly Son,_____ Was God's

on - ly Son.____ *Chorus:* Come all ye to the wil - der - ness, Glo - ry, glo - ry

be,_____ Fa - ther, Son, and the Ho - ly Ghost, Through all e - ter - ni - ty._____

The very next blessing that Mary had,
It was the blessing of two:
To know that her Son, Jesus,
Could read the Bible through,
Could read the Bible through.
(To Chorus:)

The very next blessing that Mary had,
It was the blessing of three:
To know that her Son, Jesus,
Could make the blind to see,
Could make the blind to see.
(To Chorus:)

The very next blessing that Mary had,
It was the blessing of four:
To know that her Son, Jesus,
Would live to help the poor,
Would live to help the poor.
(To Chorus:)

The very next blessing that Mary had,
It was the blessing of five:
To know that her Son, Jesus,
Could bring the dead alive,
Could bring the dead alive.
(To Chorus:)

The very next blessing that Mary had,
It was the blessing of six:
To know that her Son, Jesus,
Would bear the crucifix,
Would bear the crucifix.
(To Chorus:)

The very last blessing that Mary had,
It was the blessing of seven:
To know that her Son, Jesus,
Was safe at last in Heaven,
Was safe at last in Heaven.
(To Chorus:)

Mary counted her blessings,
She counted them one by one:
She found her greatest blessing
Was her Godly Son,
Was her Godly Son.
(To Chorus:)

Shepherd, Shake Off Your Drowsy Sleep

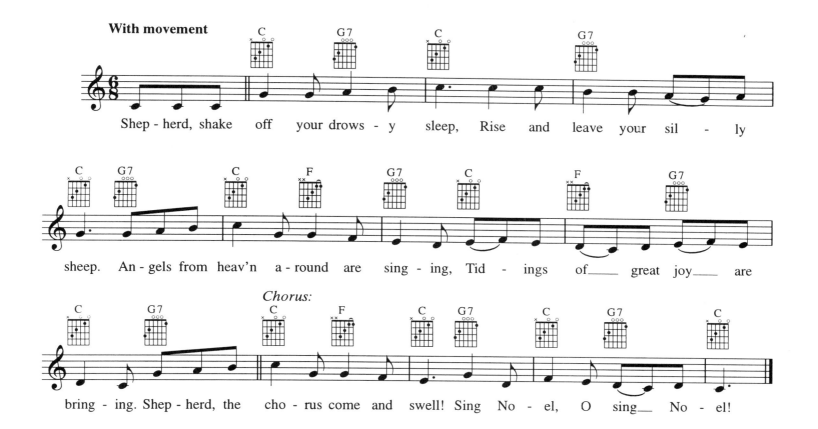

With movement

Shep - herd, shake off your drows - y sleep, Rise and leave your sil - ly

sheep. An - gels from heav'n a - round are sing - ing, Tid - ings of___ great joy___ are

Chorus:

bring - ing. Shep - herd, the cho - rus come and swell! Sing No - el, O sing___ No - el!

See how the flow'rs all burst anew,
Thinking snow is summer dew.
See how the stars afresh are glowing,
All their brightest beams bestowing.
(To Chorus:)

Shepherd, then up and quick away!
Seek the Babe ere break of day.
He is the hope of ev'ry nation,
All in Him shall find salvation.
(To Chorus:)

Shepherds To Bethlehem

(Los Pastores a Belén)

Spain

With movement

Now to Beth - le - hem are run - ning quick - ly all the shep - herds.

In a car - a - van they're com - ing, with their shoes in tat - ters.

Ay, ay, ay, with the "tam," with the "bou," With the

jing - ling tam - bou - rine and the pipes a sound - ing.

Los pastores a Belén corren presurosos,
Y todos se van en tren con zapatos rotos.
¡Ay! ¡Ay! ¡Ay! con la pan, con la de,
Con la pandereta y gaita gallega.

Silent Night

Words by Joseph Mohr
Music by Franz Gruber

Silent night, holy night,
Shepherds quake at the sight.
Glories stream from heaven afar,
Heavenly hosts sing alleluia.
Christ, the Saviour, is born!
Christ, the Saviour, is born!

Silent night, holy night,
Son of God, love's pure light.
Radiant beams from Thy holy face,
With the dawn of redeeming grace,
Jesus, Lord, at Thy birth.
Jesus, Lord, at Thy birth.

Sing-A-Lamb

Spiritual

It's young child Jesus,
Sing-a-lamb.
It's young child Jesus,
Sing-a-lamb.
It's young child Jesus,
Sing-a-lamb.

He's born in a manger,
Sing-a-lamb.
He's born in a manger,
Sing-a-lamb.
He's born in a manger,
Sing-a-lamb.
He's born in a manger,
Sing-a-lamb.

Singing In The Land

Spiritual

Praying in the land. (3)
I'm a long ways from home.
Praying in the land. (2)
Baby of Bethelehem.
(To Chorus:)

Similarly

Mourning…Preaching…Rejoicing…

0458B

Sleep, My Saviour, Sleep

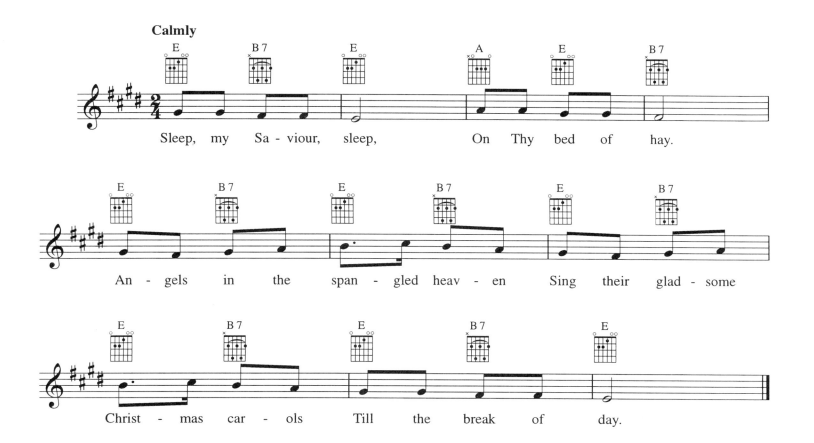

Calmly

Sleep, my Sa - viour, sleep, On Thy bed of hay.

An - gels in the span - gled heav - en Sing their glad - some

Christ - mas car - ols Till the break of day.

Sleep, my Saviour, sleep,
On Thy bed of hay.
Ere the morning Angel cometh
To the moonlit olive garden,
Wiping tears away.

Sleep, my Saviour, sleep,
Sweet on Mary's breast.
Now te shepherds kneel adoring,
Now the mother's heart is joyous,
Take Thy happy rest.

The Snow Lay On The Ground

* Come let us adore the Lord.

'Twas Mary, Virgin pure, of holy Anne,
That brought into this world the God-made man.
She laid Him in a stall in Bethlehem,
The ass and oxen share the roof with them.
(To Chorus:)

Saint Joseph, too, was by to attend the Child,
To guard Him and protect His Mother mild.
The angels hovered 'round and sang this hymn:
Venite adoremus Dominum.
(To Chorus:)

The Star Of Christmas Morning

England

We saw a light shine out a - far, On Christ - mas in the morn - ing. And straight we knew it was Christ's star, Bright beam - ing in the morn - ing. Then did we fall on bend - ed knee, On Christ - mas in the morn - ing, And praised the Lord, Who's let us see His glo - ry at its dawn - ing.

Oh! Ever thought be of His name
On Christmas in the morning,
Who bore for us both grief and shame,
Affliction's sharpest scorning.
And may we die when death shall come,
On Christmas in the morning,
And see in heav'n our glorious home,
That star of Christmas morning.

Tell Me What Month Was My Jesus Born In

Spiritual

With a bounce

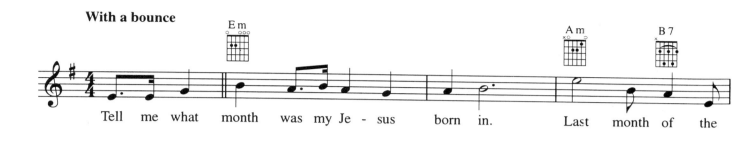

Chorus:

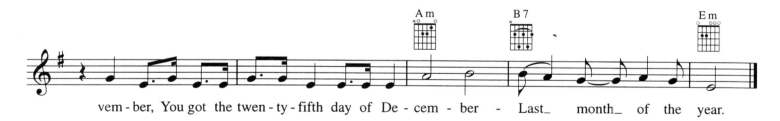

He was born in an ox-stall manger,
Last month of the year.
He was born in an ox-stall manger,
Last month of the year.
(To Chorus:)

I'm talking 'bout Mary's Baby
Last month of the year.
I'm talking 'bout Mary's Baby
Last month of the year.
(To Chorus:)

There's A Song In The Air

Moderately

There's a song in the air, there's a star in the sky, There's a moth-er's deep pray'r, and a Ba-by's low cry. And the star rains its fire,___ while the beau-ti-ful sing,___ For the man-ger of Beth-le-hem cra-dles a King!

There's a tumult of joy o'er the wonderful birth,
For the Virgin's sweet Boy is the Lord of the earth.
Ay, the star rains its fire, while the beautiful sing,
For the manger of Bethlehem cradles a King!

We rejoice in the light, and we echo the song
That comes down throught the night from the heavenly throng.
Ay, we shout to the lovely evangel they bring,
And we greet in His cradle our Saviour and King!

Today In Bethlehem

Lithuania

Moderately

Come all with sing-ing, come all with sing-ing to the place where Christ lies.

There in Beth-le-hem, there in Beth-le-hem, You shall find a man-ger.

Chorus:

Christ, Child of sto-ry, is born in glo-ry. Wise men a-dore Him,

Beasts kneel be-fore Him. Shep-herds sing-ing, pray-ing,

Stars on high o-bey-ing. O, what won-ders, won-ders to see.

There lies the Virgin, her Babe adoring,
Joseph watches near them.
Watches the Christ Child, watches the Christ Child,
The world's Redeemer.
(To Chorus:)

What have the wise men, what have the wise men
Laid before the cradle?
Gold and frankincense, gold and frankincense,
For a Kings's adorning.
(To Chorus:)

Honor and glory, honor and glory
Be unto the Father.
And to His dear Son, and to His dear Sonf,
Praises everlasting.
(To Chorus:)

Tonight A Child Is Born

Spain

With movement

On this eve - ning came an In - fant, born in - to the____ win - ter's

sting.____ If I on - ly, my dear Ba - by, could but clothe You____ like a

Chorus:

king._____ A - le rí, a - le - rí, a - le - rí - a. A - le -

rí, a - le - rí, what de - light! For to us a Child is

giv - en, born in Beth - le - hem this night.__

Oh, the Virgin, she is washing
With a little bit of soap,
And her hands are getting roughened,
Hands that hold all mankind's hope.
(To Chorus:)

The Coventry Carol

This song has four chords—but we just couldn't leave it out.

Oh, sisters too, how may we do,
For to preserve this day?
This poor Youngling for Whom we sing,
By, by, lully, lullay.

A Visit From St. Nicholas
(The Night Before Christmas)

Words by Clement Clark Moore
Music adapted by Jerry Silverman

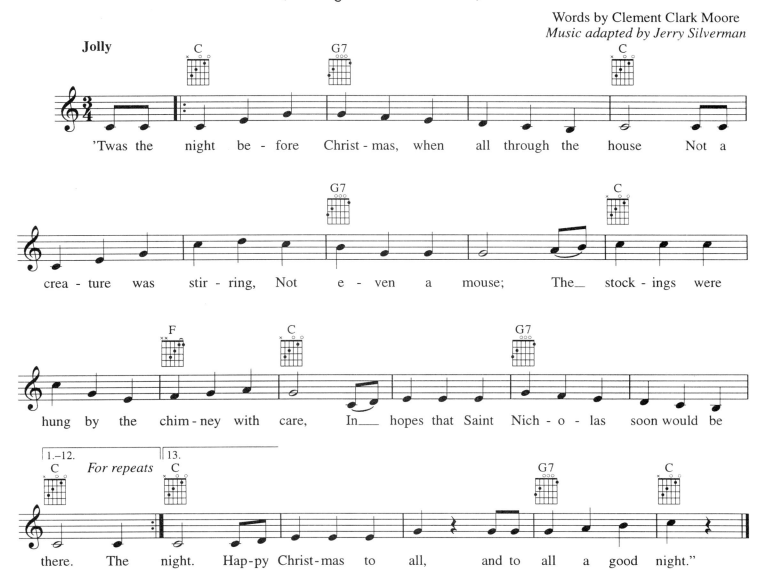

'Twas the night be - fore Christ - mas, when all through the house Not a crea - ture was stir - ring, Not e - ven a mouse; The_ stock - ings were hung by the chim - ney with care, In_ hopes that Saint Nich - o - las soon would be there. The night. Hap-py Christ-mas to all, and to all a good night."

The children were nestled all snug in their beds,
While visions of sugarplums danced in their heads;
And Mamma in her kerchief, and I in my cap,
Had just settled our brains for a long winter's nap.

When out on the lawn there arose such a clatter,
I sprang from my bed to see what was the matter.
Away to the window I flew like a flash,
Tore open the shutters aand threw up the sash.

The moon on the breast of the new-fallen snow
Gave the lustre of midday to objects below,
When, what to my wondering eyes should appear,
But a miniature sleigh, and eight tiny reindeer.

With a little old driver, so lively and quick,
I knew in a moment it must be Saint Nick.
More rapid than eagles, his coursers they came,
And he whistled, and shouted, and called them by name:

"Now, Dasher! Now, Dancer! Now, Prancer and Vixen!
On, Comet! On, Cupid! On, Donner and Blitzen!
To the top of the porch! to the top of the wall!
Now dash away! Dash away! Dash away all!"

As dry leaves that before the wild hurricane fly,
When they meet with an obstacle, mount to the sky,
So up to the house-top the coursers they flew,
With the sleigh full of toys, and Saint Nicholas too.

And then in a twinkling, I heard on the roof
The prancing and pawing of each little hoof.
As I drew in my head, and was turning around,
Down the chimney Saint Nicholas came with a bound.

The stump of a pipe he held right in his teeth,
And the smoke it encircled his head like a wreath;
He had a broad face and a round little belly,
That shook when he laughed like a bowl full of jelly.

He was chubby and plump, a right jolly old elf,
And I laughed when I saw him, in spite of myself.
A wink of his eye and a twist of his head
Soon gave me to know I had nothing to dread.

He spoke not a word, but went straight to his work,
And filled all the stockings; then turned with a jerk,
And laying his finger aside of his nose,
And giving a nod, up the chimney he rose.

He was dressed all in fur, from his head to his foot,
And his clothes were all tarnished with ashes and soot;
A bundle of toys he had flung on his back,
And he looked like a peddler just opening his pack.

His eyes, how they twinkled! His dimples how merry!
His cheeks were like roses, his nose like a cherry!
His droll little mouth was drawn up like a bow,
And the beard on his chin was as white as the snow.

He sprang to his sleigh, to his team gave a whistle,
And away they all flew like the down on a thistle.
But I heard him exclaim, ere he drove out of sight,
"Happy Christmas to all, and to all a good night.
Happy Christmas to all, and to all a good night."

Wasn't That A Mighty Day

Spiritual

With movement

Chorus:

Was-n't it a might - y day, hal - le - lu,___ hal - le - lu,___

Fine

Was-n't it a might - y day, When Je - sus Christ was born.

Verse:

Well, Je - sus was a ba - by, A - ly - ing at Ma - ry's

arm; Ly - ing in the sta - ble of Beth - le - hem,_ The beasts did keep - a Him warm.

The shepherds came to wonder,
They came from far and near.
And they saw a-lying there on the straw,
The little Child so dear.
(To Chorus:)

While Shepherds Watched Their Flocks By Night

Words by Nahum Tate
Music by George F. Handel

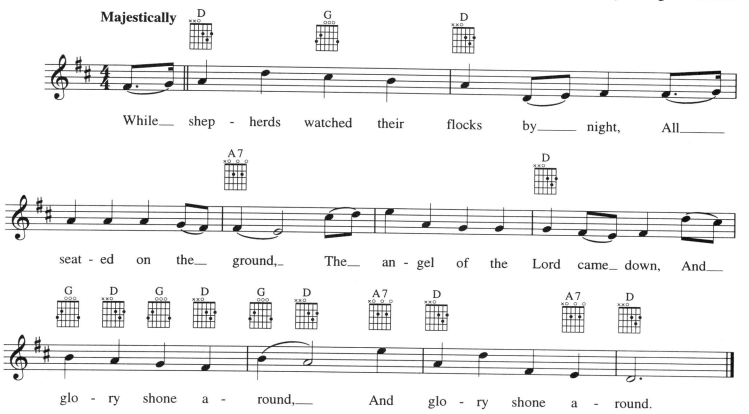

While— shep - herds watched their flocks by—— night, All——

seat - ed on the— ground,— The— an - gel of the Lord came— down, And—

glo - ry shone a - round,— And glo - ry shone a - round.

"Fear not," said he, for mighty dread
Had seized their troubled mind.
"Glad tidings of great joy I bring
To you and all mankind,
To you and all mankind."

"To you in David's town this day
Is born, of David's line,
The Saviour, Who is Christ the Lord;
And this shall be the sign,
And this shall be the sign:"

"The heav'nly Babe you there shall find
To human view displayed,
All meanly wrapped in swathing bands,
And in a manger laid,
And in a manger laid."

"All glory be to God on high,
And to the earth be peace.
Goodwill henceforth from heaven to men,
Begin and never cease,
Begin and never cease."

Yonder Comes Sister Mary

Spiritual

With movement

Yon - der comes Sis - ter Mar - y; How do you know it is her? With the

palms of vic - t'ry in her hand, And the keys of Beth - e - le - hem. And the

Chorus:

keys of Beth - e - le - hem, O Lord, The keys of Beth - e - le - hem. And the

keys of Beth - e - le - hem, O Lord, And the keys of Beth - e - le - hem.

Yonder comes Brother Joseph;
How do you know it is him?
With the palms of vict'ry in his hand,
And the keys of Bethelehem.
(To Chorus:)

Yonder comes Baby Jesus;
How do you know it is Him?
With the palms of vict'ry in his hand,
And the keys of Bethelehem.
(To Chorus:)

0458B